DEAD TRUE CRIME

MURDERER'S
GULCH

Carnage in the Catskills

C.J. MARCH

SLINGSHOT
BOOKS

New York, 1893

Prologue

The women disembarked on the island and took a last look at freedom. Behind them, across the salty expanse of the East River, lay Manhattan's castles of industry, its gracious uptown mansions and parks, the immigrant neighborhoods mushrooming downtown. The boat trip hadn't been a long one—maybe a few hundred meters of tidal current—but they might as well have traveled a thousand miles from New York City, from life itself. They clambered into the horse-drawn ambulance that met them at the landing and turned their eyes to the long, granite building waiting for them up ahead.

As they drove up, a nauseating stench from the kitchen building greeted them. Nellie Bly covered her face. Torn between elation at her success at having infiltrated the Women's Lunatic Asylum on Blackwell's Island posing as a madwoman and anxiety at what lay inside those stone walls, Bly paused at the dread on the other women's faces. She would be getting out in ten days; her editor at the *New York World* had sworn when he gave her the assignment. Her companions on the trip over would probably never leave.

Bly was thrust into a cell with six women but had to count herself lucky—other cells held as many as ten. The conditions were squalid. A once-a-week bath used the same water for inmate after inmate until it resembled thick sludge. They shared a towel among them, including those with infectious sores. Nurses routinely beat the women. Bly herself sustained injuries, including two broken ribs. Women were choked, held underwater till they lost consciousness, had their heads bashed against the walls. The institution gave them "so much morphine and chloral that the patients were made crazy." The drugs made them "wild for water," which the nurses then denied them. Bly cried for water until her mouth was so dry she couldn't speak. It was hell.

The series of articles Nellie Bly wrote about the brutal, even torturous, conditions she experienced firsthand in those ten days, later published as the book *Ten Days in a Mad-House*, met critical and popular acclaim. They also led to significant changes in New York City's Department of Public Charities and Correction. But her experience going undercover as a madwoman may also have prepared her to interview one of the most dangerous women in the world.

By the time Bly met her, Lizzie Halliday single-handedly murdered possibly dozens of people, using methods unthinkable at the time for a woman. The question of whether these were crimes of madness or of a cold, evil sanity would dog the criminal justice system, and Lizzie would bounce between prison and asylum over the course of her career. She may never have experienced quite the hellish conditions the journalist did on Blackwell's Island, though. And that's in part thanks to Bly herself.

The two asylums Lizzie would spend time in were experiments in the "new" model of managing the mentally ill. Opened in the years following the exposé, Middletown and Matteawan were institutions intended to promote health and sanity, rather than just contain and beat down insanity. The reality fell well short of the intention but was a step on the path to reform.

By the time Lizzie Halliday, the woman the *New York Times* called "the worst woman on earth," was done killing, even Blackwell's Island may have seemed too good for her. For the very reforms Bly's exposé helped to bring about—the relative freedom inmates could experience in the new asylums, the attachments they could make with their keepers—would give Lizzie Halliday just the opening she needed to stab a nurse two hundred times with scissors.

People traveled from miles around to settle their disputes at the picturesque stone courthouse in Monticello. The seat of Sullivan County, Monticello was a quiet town a hundred miles from both Albany and New York City—a five-day trip by horse and wagon. Before Lizzie Halliday's trial, the cases Sullivan County's citizens brought to that courthouse tended to be "disputes about a boundary marked by a tottering stone wall . . . or lawsuits concerning the broken wheel of a wagon."

Sullivan County is a nearly one thousand square mile area in the Catskill Mountains in southeastern New York State, part of the Hudson River valley. Depicted in the paintings of the nineteenth century Hudson River school, site of the 1969 Woodstock Festival, and bed to the fictional Rip Van Winkle, the Catskills are well represented in the American cultural imagination. In the early twentieth century, the area was home to the Borscht Belt (also known as the Jewish Alps), summer resorts popular with Eastern European immigrants. From the 1920s to the 1970s, Jewish entertainers, including Henny Youngman, Buddy Hackett, Woody Allen, and Joan Rivers, honed their acts there. Famed prizefighters like Rocky Marciano, Muhammad Ali, and Sonny Liston trained there.

As early as 1872, Sullivan County newspaper publisher Hamilton Child wrote of his home county that the "quiet and attractive scenery . . . is becoming appreciated by the lovers of the beautiful in nature, and those who seek a retreat from the heat and dust of the cities in summer, and a brief respite from the cares and perplexities of business." The mountains and lakes of Sullivan County attracted thousands of summer visitors, and the citizens relied on temporary workers both for the influx of tourists and for farming help. It's possible that people at first took little notice of a new housekeeper at the Halliday farm.

Paul Halliday, known as "Old Paul," farmed III acres in Sullivan County just outside of Burlingham. "One of the oldest residents of the region," Paul was well-liked by his neighbors, and though considered "close fisted," they found him honest. When he drank, which wasn't often, he could be quarrelsome, and at seventy years old "he could hold his own at fisticuffs with almost any one in that part of the country." He'd fought in the Civil War in Company K of the 124th Regiment, widely known as the "Orange Blossom" regiment, whose experiences purportedly informed Stephen Crane's novel *The Red Badge of Courage*.

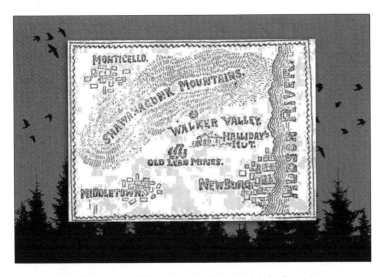

Hand drawn map of the area surrounding the Halliday farm, 1893.

Paul spent the early part of his life in Ulster in Ireland, but after the death of his first wife came to the United States and married four more times. His second marriage lasted just a year; this wife spent her last days at the Women's Lunatic Asylum on Blackwell's Island—the same institution where Nellie Bly went undercover. Not much is known about her, or what led to her commitment to Blackwell's. Another of his American wives died of consumption, and "Old Paul," refusing to pay for a funeral, dug a grave on "unconsecrated ground" and buried her. The six children from these marriages grew up, married, and lived in the region, except for his son John, who stayed on with Paul on the farm.

In 1890, sometime after his last wife died, Paul went looking for a housekeeper. In Newburgh, at an employment agency (called "intelligence offices" back then), he met Lizzie Brown. She had recently applied there, claiming she had just arrived in the country.

One paper described her as "above medium height and of stout, muscular build . . . [with] cinnamon colored hair and a skin so fair that it makes her somewhat plain face look handsomer than it really is." Another publication claimed that she "had but one charm of person, a beautiful complexion," and that her hair was red, "her eyes were small with a disagreeable expression of low cunning, her mouth was large and coarse, and her nose was like a snout." A neighbor said she was a short, thick-set woman with a repulsive face, and the most peculiar nose he'd ever seen. He also said that she had "great muscular strength."

Newspaper artist drawing of Lizzie Halliday, 1893.

When Paul was introduced to Lizzie, she questioned the farmer in a "mighty business-like way," learning that he had rheumatism, owned a large farm and a mill, and had a veteran's pension. Lizzie would turn out to have an attraction to old soldiers with pensions. Paul Halliday and Lizzie Brown were from the same county in Ireland and their families knew each other there—another reason he may have hired her so quickly. She immediately moved in with Paul and his son John on the hundred acres of land. The pitched-roofed Halliday house had one story and only two rooms; the humble structure was often referred to as a shanty. An orchard, a potato patch, and the surrounding swamp and woods made it difficult to see from the road. Only three weeks after Lizzie moved in with him as his housekeeper, they were married by a Methodist minister and she took Paul Halliday's name. She was his sixth wife. He may have believed that he was her first husband.

Some thought that the older man had married his young housekeeper so he would no longer have to pay her a salary. If so, those few pinched pennies cost him dearly. His eldest son, Robert, claimed that "she had a peculiar influence over him which nothing could shake," that his father "was infatuated with her." The loyalty the farmer showed her through and after her many crimes suggests Robert may have been right. None of the family liked her and they worried about the marriage from the start.

Dislike of Lizzie extended to the people of the small community. One neighbor said that she met her frequently in the countryside, but that Lizzie "averted her face so as to avoid recognizing her." The neighbor "warned her children not to go into her house, because she distrusted her."

There were rumors about Lizzie's past—that she was or had been a Gypsy queen. Some gossiped that before her marriage to Paul Halliday, she had been the leader of a small band of "gipsies" that roamed the Hudson and Mohawk Valleys. Her merry band of travelers, they said, had held a short celebration of Paul and Lizzie's marriage, elected another queen, and moved along.

Mentions of Gypsy influences and involvement appear frequently in the coverage of Lizzie. Speculation that she was aided in her crimes by Gypsies that "headquartered" in the region made it into the papers. There was even a report, when Lizzie was finally arrested, that "gypsies would attempt to rescue her from the officers of the law." There's little evidence she actually had any meaningful interaction with the Romany or any other itinerant group. People may have tried to make sense of the extent and brutality of her crimes by asserting that a woman could not have killed in the manner she did without help. But the references also seem to point to racism and xenophobia, and the need to associate her with a group believed to be dangerous or "other."

In 1906, George N. Olcott wrote a long article in the New-York Tribune called, "The Ways of the Gipsy." "But the Gipsies! We do not, cannot, understand them. We despise them as worthless vagabonds; and they despise us too, even as they amuse us, and fool us sometimes." He calls them "unknown and mysterious." It was typical of the sentiment and coverage of the time.

The marriage was purported to be a rocky one from the start. The *New York Times* stated, mildly, "their married life does not seem to be pleasant." Paul told his son that Lizzie was prone to "spells of insanity" that were "particular to women." His children urged him to get rid of her. That he didn't, that her "spells" over the next two years grew only more vicious and criminal, would ultimately be the end of Paul Halliday.

The fate of Paul's son John should have been a warning to the old farmer. The only one of Paul's children left on the farm, John suffered from a mental or physical disability. One brother referred to him as "crippled." He was also described as "half crazy," "Paul's idiot son," and "half witted." At thirty-five years old, he was not much younger than Lizzie when she became his stepmother.

The neighbors knew that Lizzie didn't like John and didn't want him around. But no one in the sleepy little hamlet could have anticipated just how far she'd go to get rid of him. Lizzie and Paul had been married less than a year when Paul Halliday returned home to find that, in his absence, a building described in various reports as either the family mill or the family cabin had burned to the ground. He searched the property for his family and found only his wife, Lizzie, sitting as placidly and contentedly in the barn as if she were in her own parlor. The neighbors said that they saw her sitting on a trunk, watching the flames. When he asked her where John had gone, Lizzie merely grinned and pointed to the charred ashes of their family home.

Paul searched the ruins for his poor son and found a body, charred beyond recognition. The neighbors suspected that Lizzie had locked John in his room, then took a torch to the house with him inside it. Paul's other sons believed that she had killed him first, possibly with an ax, and used the fire to cover up the murder.

Lizzie was immediately arrested, but she denied involvement and since there was no direct evidence linking her to the arson or John's death, she went free. A plea of insanity may have played a role in her release. Meanwhile, her husband began rebuilding the house.

Two weeks later, Lizzie burned down the barn. This time, she admitted to Paul that she started the fire because the barn was old and she wanted a new one. Both the house and barn were insured, and the claims were paid by the insurance company. This was not the first time that she had committed arson for insurance money, but Paul didn't know that.

Around this time, Lizzie also admitted to him that she had been married before. She told him that she didn't like her first husband, so, when he was asleep, she killed him with a "big stone" and then mutilated his body.

None of these events or confessions prompted Paul to evict or divorce Lizzie. Instead, he attributed her violent and erratic behavior to "a condition peculiar to married women" and claimed that when she "got rid of the physical cause of her spells of insanity," she "resumed her normal conditions of life." His euphemisms likely referred to menstruation or pregnancy. If Paul was attributing arson and murder to either, it reflected a stunning misunderstanding female physiology perhaps not uncommon at the time and a tragic misjudgment of his wife's capacity for destruction.

Still, Paul began to keep a record of what he called "Lizzie Halliday's crime" in a memorandum book. Entries included documentation of the fires: "May 6, 1891, the house was burned" and "Burnt barn May 26, 1891." He also borrowed a revolver from a man who boarded near the farm.

Lizzie's behavior caused some to suspect her of other crimes, as well, but it wasn't until her murder trial that neighbors reflected on the disappearances and killings in the area. They speculated on her role in the mysterious disappearance of a four-teen-year-old boy. And a year earlier, on a Sunday morning in the summer of 1890 (shortly after their marriage), a man was walking several miles from the Halliday farm when his straw hat blew off and landed at the mouth of an abandoned lead mine. Inside, near the entrance, he found a body lying face down in a pool of water.

The man in the mine had been shot through the back of his head and when the walker turned the body over, a "bullet of large calibre" fell out of its mouth. The body was of a peddler "consid-ered well off for one of his craft"; the motive believed to be robbery. At first, the Gypsies were blamed for the murder.

Peddlers were critical to trade, wandering with their packs over the countryside, providing supplies to the towns and farms. When night came, they would often stop at the nearest house or farm and either pay for a night's lodging or rely on hospitality. "More often they are given a bed and a cordial welcome, as the peddlers generally have a fund of anecdotes and stories and the news from town to tell."

During the Nellie Bly interviews after her arrest, Lizzie would provide a litany of convoluted stories in which she had witnessed, but not participated in, the murders. In a rambling tale of a robbing and murdering gang, she claimed to be an eyewitness to the killing of peddlers. Her accounts were disjointed and strange but included specific details that were unintentionally self-incrim-inating, details suggesting she was responsible for those deaths. The Hallidays would have entertained many peddlers over the years, and, at one point in her time with Bly, Lizzie "cheerfully asserts that for some of them it was their last night on earth." The mountains around the Halliday farm were full of abandoned mineshafts that may have held the bodies of travelers who had the misfortune to cross paths with Lizzie.

Despite what he knew or suspected about her, Paul considered Lizzie "the most wonderful woman he had ever met." A startling contrast to the *New York Times* contention that she was the "worst woman on earth." Lizzie, however, may not have considered him the most wonderful man she had ever met.

Less than a year after burning down the house and barn, she made plans to leave Paul. Lizzie hired a wagon and a team of horses from a livery stable in Newburgh and convinced a man in the area, John Glynn, "an old, red-whiskered fellow," to join her, telling him that she would pay him $1 a day to drive the team. The plan was to pose as husband and wife and go from town to town, trading the horses as they traveled, and "getting the best of the trade on each deal, until eventually they both became rich." The owner of the livery went after them and, with difficulty, recovered his horses and wagon from the people that Lizzie and Glynn had sold them to, who many newspapers claimed were "some gypsies." The pair were eventually caught and arrested.

As soon as she was jailed, Lizzie began to "act violently." The jail physician promptly declared her insane. When Paul arrived, he "expressed great contempt" for the diagnosis, maintaining that his wife was "perfectly sane and that she was simply acting like a crazy woman to escape punishment." In the years to come, Lizzie's mental competence would come under scrutiny any number of times by the newspapers, by lawyers, and by the public. Was she in control of her faculties and pretending madness when she was caught? Or was her violence pathological evidence of criminal insanity?

When Lizzie was brought before the court on the charge of horse stealing, she "shrieked and cried and raved and tore her hair." The judge agreed with the jail physician that she was insane and acquitted her of the criminal charge. She was first remanded to the Middletown asylum, and then moved to the newly built Matteawan Hospital for the Criminally Insane. She'd get to know Matteawan well.

Lizzie spent two years in Matteawan but was released as "cured" at Paul Halliday's request. Paul's son Robert begged his father to leave the woman, but he refused. If the report by towns-folk of Lizzie driving a team of horses as fast as she could down the road, shouting that the devils were after her is true, then the cure that Paul or her doctors hoped for didn't take. Then, in August 1893, Paul Halliday disappeared.

Neighbors and townsfolk noticed Paul's absence immediately. The old farmer went back and forth to town frequently and was friendly with his neighbors; "the gossip he garnered was greatly relished." It seems as though he was liked as much as Lizzie was not. So, when no one saw him for several days, people began to wonder what had happened to him. He had last been seen on Wednesday, August 30. At first, folks wondered if he was sick, but as time passed, they worried about his safety. His sons were sent for to check on him. On Saturday morning, September 2, they found Lizzie, "cleaning house and singing while she worked."

Paul had gone away for a few days to Burlingham, Lizzie told them, to make payment on a piece of land. Paul was a talkative sort, and no one believed that he would be working on a land deal without having mentioned it to anyone. Pretending to believe her, the sons left and met up with a couple of neighbors who insisted on returning with them to the farm and further questioning Lizzie, "who stuck to her story without wincing."

The only way to figure out what was going on was to stake out the farm, the men decided. They hunkered down and watched it for the remainder of the weekend, but never saw Paul. On Monday morning, September 4, one of the sons visited Lizzie to ask again after his father. Not knowing that she'd been watched, she told him that Paul had spent Sunday with her but had left again for Burlingham that morning. Suspicion ran high and concern for Paul was escalating.

They went to Burlingham to check on her story and learned that Paul hadn't been seen there since the previous Wednesday. Returning to the Halliday farm, they picked up Constable Scott on the way. This time, questioned about her husband's disappearance, Lizzie lost her temper. "Grabbing a hoary club she ordered them from the house." The men pushed past her and, in the bedroom, found a lit lantern next to bedding and clothing that were "saturated with coal oil." They suspected that she intended to burn the house down to hide the murder of her husband. But they still had no proof.

Lizzie held to her story and, in a cooler temper, "offered with apparent good humor" to go with Constable Scott to Burlingham to find her husband. Meanwhile, the others searched the house but found no indications of foul play. They continued to the barn and haymow and were about to give up when one of them noticed fresh hay in a cow pen near a manure pile. Paul was "too prudent" to toss good hay away like that. They got pitchforks and moved the pile to reveal an area covered in a packed layer of straw and manure—what they suspected was the man's grave. When they began digging, they uncovered a human foot. They removed more manure and dirt to reveal the rest of a body. Instead of Paul Halliday, though, they found the corpse of a young woman.

Turning over the body, they saw that she was bound at the wrists, knees, and ankles. In removing the woman from the trench, they found another body underneath her; the body of an older woman bound and wrapped in rags like the first. They continued to dig, expecting to find Paul's body as well, but it wasn't there. When the house was searched again with an eye to the deaths of the two women, their clothing was found—"a complete outfit and all of fine material . . . evidently belonged to the young woman," and "a lot of clothing of a poorer quality, which belonged to the older woman."

Word was sent to the justice and coroner, and to Constable Scott, who was being led around Burlingham by Lizzie Halliday in the search for her husband. She was "cool and good humored; even merry at times." When the messenger caught up with them, Scott immediately arrested her, taking her back to his house for holding until they could make the trip to the county seat and the jail there.

Lizzie said, "Humph, I know nothing at all about any two women." Shortly after her arrest, though, she displayed symptoms of one of her "spells of insanity," and reported seeing frogs, lizards, and snakes, and screamed and tore off her clothing. She was shackled, and, according to one newspaper article, "continued to jabber like a crazy woman, though when she thinks she is not observed she steals covert glances at her keepers as if to see how her frenzy affects them."

When Paul Halliday rebuilt the barn Lizzie burned down because she wanted a new one, he never could have imagined the scene that would unfold inside. The police laid out the bodies and body parts of the two women, and there, surrounded by hay and manure and Paul's farm implements, three doctors performed the post-mortem examination. They found that the younger woman had been shot seven times and the older woman, eight, both in the heart. Scorch marks on the breasts of the women showed that the murderer held the muzzle of the gun against their chests. Other than the bullet wounds, there were no other marks or bruises on the women. The deaths appeared to be executions.

The news "spread like wildfire." Strange now in this age of police tape and sealed investigations, hundreds came to see the bodies, but no one recognized them and many speculated that they were summer boarders, not from the area.

Descriptions of the women's garments in a local newspaper led to their identification. Margaret McQuillan, fifty years old, and Sarah McQuillan, nineteen years old, were from Newburgh, a full day's wagon trip away from the Halliday farm. They were the wife and daughter of Thomas McQuillan, a gardener and laborer. It wouldn't be until deep into the trial that their relationship to Lizzie and their path to the Halliday farm would be laid bare. And when Paul's body still could not be found, a new theory regarding his disappearance was briefly entertained—that he had helped his wife kill the women and then fled.

The police interviewed people in surrounding towns and searchers scoured the farm, "prying into every corner, ripping up the floor, and examining the earth without success." Lizzie stuck to her story that Paul had gone away. It took a reluctant neighbor to find him.

Photographs of the barn where McQuillan women were buried, 1893.

Charles Greve, a real estate dealer from Brooklyn, spent his summers at the farm next to the Halliday's. Planning to return to the city shortly, he had wanted to avoid involvement in the case and the long winter in Sullivan County that being a witness would mean. Yet, like many neighbors, he was aware of Lizzie's strange behavior, and prompted by his respect and esteem for Paul, he went onto the Halliday farm in the middle of the night to investigate.

Bringing a crowbar, he entered the house and examined the floorboards. One didn't match; it had been "taken up and put down differently." Either it had been missed by the previous searches or disregarded. Prying up the board, he discovered soft earth recently disturbed. He let the crowbar sink into the soil and it "dropped without effort until it touched something." Greve was stunned. He immediately sent word to Burlingham; the police came and took over the second crime scene on the farm. Digging into the soil under the floorboards, they removed eighteen inches of dirt to reveal Paul Halliday's face.

The next afternoon, with the coroner present, they laid out Paul Halliday's body on a table. "His head had been battered with a club or gunstock. There was a contusion on the left side of the face and the eye hung down upon the cheek." He had been shot in the heart three times. The pistol used to kill him and the women was soon found concealed in an ash barrel. It was the one Paul had borrowed for protection.

After that week's grim discoveries, the farm would come to be called "Murderer's Gulch."

4

Eliza "Lizzie" Margaret McNally was born at a time known by the Irish as "An Drochshaol," literally, "The Bad Life." Often referred to outside of Ireland as the "Irish Potato Famine," the period Ireland itself called the "Great Famine" or "Great Hunger" was one of mass starvation and disease; more than a million people died and a million more emigrated from Ireland, causing the population to fall by over 20 percent. Though the "Great Famine" was officially considered over by 1849, its effects were felt long into the twentieth century.

The youngest of nine siblings, Lizzie left County Antrim in the Ulster province of Ireland with her family for the United States a few years after her 1864 birth. Paul Halliday, who knew her mother, Peggy Brown, had left Ireland years before Lizzie was born. The McNally family were among many County Antrim families of their acquaintance who emigrated during the 1800s. Families like the McQuillans, whom Lizzie would encounter again in the New World.

The McNallys likely sailed from Belfast, the major seaport in County Antrim, on a "coffin ship," an overloaded vessel in poor condition. "Coffin ships" were deliberately over-insured and so, more valuable if they sank. Thirty percent mortality rates were common, and it was said that sharks could be seen following the ships, so many bodies were thrown overboard. The trip took from forty days to three months. Lizzie was three when she arrived in the United States in 1867.

There are no detailed records of her childhood or early adulthood, but Lizzie must have faced profound challenges as an Irish immigrant, and as a girl and woman during the 1860s and 1870s, which often meant marrying young.

Indeed, Lizzie McNally married her first husband when she was only fifteen years old. Far older than his bride, Charles Hopkins was known to most as "Ketspool Brown," an alias he used after deserting from the army. With him, she had one child, a son, who was twelve at the time of the trial and living in a Pennsylvania institution much like the hospital for the insane where she herself would eventually end up. Hopkins died a couple of years after his marriage to Lizzie. She contended that he died of typhoid fever, but Ketspool may have been her first victim.

She moved into a two-room apartment above a blacksmith shop and took work as a washerwoman. She quickly married Artemas Brewer, a "broken down veteran," who reportedly endured "beatings and hair pullings" from her. Lizzie called him a "bad old man," and said that he chewed opium, "same as Chinamen smoke." Whenever his rheumatism flared, she took pleasure in making him go outside to chop wood. He died a year later. According to Lizzie, the cause was "dropsy of the heart."

Her third husband was Hiram Parkinson, another man she met while working as a washerwoman. With a long, white beard and mustache, he resembled a "deacon in a country church." According to some reports, he deserted her within their first year of marriage. Lizzie claimed she found out that the stonemason was already married and she kicked him out. It's also possible he left the area for work, not considering the marriage to be over.

Without divorcing Parkinson, she took another husband. Her fourth was as old as her first three, possibly the oldest. George Smith also took his wash to Lizzie and, within weeks of meeting him, she urged him to marry her. Smith had been a friend of her previous late husband, Brewer. He demurred, as it was a "serious matter," and "besides that," he said, "you're married to Hi Parkinson." She told Smith that she would take an oath that she had never been married to Parkinson, which she did in the presence of a lawyer. Of the union, Lizzie said "he was an old soldier and drew a pension, so I married him." She later served him a cup of tea laced with poison, and "laughingly left him writhing on the floor." When Smith didn't die, she escaped to Bellows Falls, Vermont, taking with her every item of his that could be construed as valuable and selling them as she could. George Smith didn't pursue her. "I thought I was lucky to escape with my life," he said.

In Vermont, she married Charles Playstel, "the only man on her list that could be called young." Playstel, a painter and paperhanger by trade, was also the only one of her husbands of whom Lizzie spoke with "the slightest sign of warmth or fondness." Yet, the theme of money and gain continued in her narrative about this marriage: "He was a lovely husband; he always gave all his money to me."

Her marriage to Playstel was shorter than any previous, lasting only two weeks before Lizzie deserted him. The reason she gave for leaving was Playstel's admission that he had "pounded his first wife to death." Lizzie disappeared for a couple of years, possibly staying with her mother or keeping house for her brother or working for friends of the family. After her arrest, a theory cropped up that she had committed a series of horrific murders in Whitechapel, London, during this unaccounted for time.

When she appeared once more with her son, it was in Philadelphia, in the winter of 1888. Recalling that members of the McQuillan family, a clan who'd lived near the McNallys in Ireland, had settled in Philadelphia, she first went to John McQuillan's saloon and home at 1218 North Front Street in the Fishtown neighborhood. (Local legend held that Charles Dickens, during a visit in March 1842, had named the area for the shad fishing industry on the nearby Delaware River.) Lizzie asked the McQuillans if she could stay with them, "on the plea of old family friendship." None of them could know that, just a few years later, she would shoot to death two of their New York cousins.

Not far from the McQuillan's saloon, Lizzie set up a shop at 2840 Kensington Avenue, which she insured on the "ten cents a week" installment premium plan. She sold fruit and candles and took in washing. During the lunch hour, she offered soup and rolls. Then she burned it down for the insurance money. The houses of two neighbors burned with it. For this crime, her son was taken away from her and Lizzie was sentenced to two years at the Eastern State Penitentiary in Pennsylvania, her first arrest and incarceration.

When she was released, in poor clothes and without anything to her name, starting over yet again, she moved to Newburgh, NY, into the home of Mrs. J.H. Smith, a Newburgh "intelligence officer," a sort of resource-finder for both employment-seekers and employers.

During the initial few weeks of her first job, working for a Mrs. Vaughan, she stayed away all night for two nights. She was suspected of being out at the "gypsy camps" in the neighborhood —possibly the first, but not the last, time public fear of Gypsies would mythologize Lizzie's story. After a month of working for Mrs. Vaughan, she asked for other employment. Just at the time a widower farmer they called "Old Paul," used to having a woman around to keep up the place, came looking for a housekeeper.

5

By the time she arrived at the Sullivan County jail to be held until her trial for the murder of Paul Halliday and the McQuillan women, Lizzie Halliday looked more like a worn traveler in need of a hot meal than a serial murderer about to be brought to justice. She'd had an uncomfortable journey from Burlingham to the jail in Monticello, over twenty-five miles in the back of a wagon, escorted by Constable Scott. She wore "an old calico waist of polka-dot blue, and a skirt of woolen, red and white mixed."

The Sullivan County jail had housed prisoners in the past, but none quite like this one. This was a "community of plain and quiet people, where crime is almost unknown." A curious crowd had gathered around the jail to see Lizzie. They might have been expecting a demon with wild eyes, still coated in the blood of her kills and lunging at anyone with a pulse. What they saw instead was a silent young woman who was escorted without resistance into the jail. Little was then known about Lizzie, the details of her past and the murders still to be revealed during the investigation and trial. Over the next few months, she denied her involvement and alternated between recalcitrant silence and displays of apparent madness.

A *New York Times* reporter attempted an interview with Lizzie Halliday shortly after her arrest, but "her language was incoherent." When it seemed evident that she couldn't be understood and there was no indication that her behavior would change, the interview ended. Several accounts imply that she simply learned to act crazy from her previous time spent at Matteawan Hospital for the Criminally Insane, and in a cold and calculating attempt to save herself from facing justice, imitated those who were truly ill. Lizzie Halliday had even bragged to neighbors that she was perfectly capable of faking a manic state. More likely, Lizzie's belief in her own control of her mental state was yet another delusion.

Nearly a year would pass between her arrest and her trial. She spent that entire time in the Monticello jail under the supervision of Sheriff Harrison Beecher, his wife, and the prison staff. Over the months, periods of silence and calm were punctuated by spells of yelling and attempts at physical violence—both to those around her and to herself. Her health also seemed to markedly deteriorate. Only a few weeks after she was arrested, she "looked weak from her sickness and imprisonment, her face being of ashy paleness"—this, in contrast to descriptions of her previous robustness and strength.

Lizzie displayed no remorse or horror about the murders; instead, she inquired into "all the details with evident interest." It didn't help public opinion that she showed "none of the grief and excitement" expected of someone who was innocent of the murder of three people. Beecher worked to extract a confession from her in her more lucid moments, but he was unable to get her to drop her guard. She often bragged of her "skill in assuming various characters and of her self control."

One day, months after her arrest, the sheriff's wife entered Lizzie's cell to tidy up or engage the prisoner in conversation. To her, Lizzie "seemed to be in a quiet frame of mind." But when Mrs. Beecher turned her back on the prisoner, Lizzie caught her by the throat and pulled her backward toward the floor. Before Lizzie could kill Mrs. Beecher, a jailer came to the rescue, helping her escape the cell. Once again, the authorities debated whether this was a calculated attempt at escape, or one of her "spells of insanity."

After the failed strangling, Lizzie went on a hunger strike. She would sometimes take a little milk from the sheriff, of whom she seemed to be fond, but would grow sullen if anyone else offered her food or drink. With her health rapidly failing from her self-imposed starvation, she was eventually force-fed by nasal tube. The jailhouse physician "pumped food into her stomach for four days under a strong protest on her part."

Lizzie wasn't done just because her attempts to starve herself failed. With winter coming, and no other means to heat her cell, a coal stove had been put in with her. Biding her time, she lit the bedclothes with the burning coals, hoping to burn the jail down. Anticipating something like this, the sheriff had "placed a barrel of water in close proximity to the cell door, and with the aid of the jail assistants the fire was extinguished."

MRS. HALLIDAY IN HANDCUFFS.

Newspaper engraving of Halliday, 1893.

Unable to escape or burn down the jail, Lizzie turned again to suicide. Using pieces of glass she'd broken from the prison window, she cut her own throat. She succeeded in making several large gashes before she was discovered by Sheriff Beecher; she'd also cut her arms and other places on her body. When she was asked why she had cut herself, she said "she wanted to see if she would bleed." Her other known suicide attempt was by self-strangulation with her own garter.

She removed it from her leg, managed to clip it open, and tried to garotte herself with it. Again, she was stopped before she could complete the job. The jail staff were changing their opinion of Lizzie Halliday's sanity: now, they believed that "this unfortunate woman has periods when she is not accountable for what she does."

Finally, driven to save both her life and the lives of everyone in the jail, including his own wife, Sheriff Harrison Beecher had Lizzie chained to the floor by a large ring in the center of the room.

By this time, Sheriff Beecher had begun to construct a theory about his violent prisoner. As strange as Lizzie Halliday's behavior was and as calculated and brutal as her murders would appear to be, it was a stretch to link her to a series of horrific killings over three thousand miles away in London. But this is just what the sheriff and a handful of papers would do.

In September 1888, after Lizzie left Charles Playstel in Vermont, but before she appeared in Philadelphia, London was terrorized by a series of brutal murders in the neighborhoods of Whitechapel and the Spitalfields. This killer, nameless throughout the spree of disemboweling and throat slashing, would later be known to the larger world as Jack the Ripper. The Ripper was believed to have murdered at least five women during that bloody fall. Sheriff Beecher and a few reporters attempted to pin these slayings on Lizzie Halliday. Where, after all, had she been that autumn before she turned up on John McQuillan's doorstep? And hadn't Lizzie proven herself amply capable of such monstrous brutality as demonstrated in the London murders?

Of the five murders that can be credibly connected to Jack the Ripper, the first four occurred within about a month's time in September, then another in late November of the same year. Many of the murdered women were prostitutes and all lived in lower socioeconomic conditions: workhouse women, impoverished women, women who belonged to the slums and "rookeries" of central London.

A carman discovered the first victim's body in a narrow lane on the way to work. Mary Ann Nichols' throat had been deeply slashed and a large incision made into her stomach. She had been killed at the site just thirty minutes before she was found.

The next woman, Annie Chapman, was discovered a week

later not far from the first. Her throat had been slit in just the same manner, but she had also been disemboweled and her intestines thrown across her shoulders. The killer took her uterus and parts of her vagina and bladder. The divisional surgeon devoted to the investigation believed that the mutilations and cuts were "the work of an expert"—possibly a doctor or fellow surgeon.

The next two murders occurred on a single night, a high point of terror for the city and an escalation in the Ripper's already brutal crimes. The first woman to die that September night was Elizabeth Stride. When she was discovered at 1 a.m., blood was just beginning to coagulate from the slash in her throat and her body was still warm. She was not mutilated. This detail, as well as the differences in the cut profile, caused some to argue that she was not a Ripper victim. Others suspected that the killer was simply interrupted. If Jack was interrupted, was that what drove the brutality of the next slaughter?

Catherine Eddowes was within walking distance from where Elizabeth Stride was found. Her death occurred less than an hour later. Her face was savagely mutilated, her intestines were tucked over her shoulder, and the disembowelment was particularly gruesome. This time, the slasher took a kidney. The speed at which the murders had to have happened underlined the killer's expertise with a knife.

Several weeks later, George Lusk, head of a volunteer patrol group called the Whitechapel Vigilance Committee, received the infamous "From Hell" letter, considered the most legitimate letter (of an untold number of hoaxes) sent during that autumn of terror. It was slipped in with a small package that contained a piece of a human kidney, and the message "Catch me when you can." The organ, preserved in wine spirits, was originally thought to be either the prank of a medical student or the kidney of a sheep and was not taken seriously until a doctor was brought in to do an examination. The kidney appeared to be from Catherine

Eddowes, or at least another woman who was forty-five and an alcoholic at the time of her death, three weeks prior to the receipt of the kidney.

Then, in late November, Mary Jane Kelly was murdered. She was found in her room by a lodging housekeeper's assistant sent to collect the rent. The ashes in the fireplace were still warm. She was wearing only a chemise. As with the other women, her throat was slashed and her abdomen ripped open. But the killer didn't stop there. One of her arms had been detached and her legs had been hacked and placed at right angles. Both of her breasts and her nose had been cut off, and other parts of her body were skinned and mutilated. Her uterus, one of her breasts, and her kidney had been placed under her head. Her chest had been ripped into and her heart carved out. Her face had been so badly cut up as to be unrecognizable.

A photographer arrived and took pictures of the scene, including Mary Jane Kelly's eyes. A theory at the time speculated that, when someone was killed violently, the last images were permanently captured on the retina. This theory was the inspiration for Jules Verne's story "Les Frères Knap." Kelly's eyes, unfortunately, did not help identify her killer, but hers would be the last murder attributed to Jack the Ripper. It was assumed after the fact that he was institutionalized, arrested for another crime, died, or moved away from the area. He was never caught.

Some, though, believed that he was a she, and that she immigrated to Newburgh, New York and married Paul Halliday. Sheriff Harrison Beecher fervently believed this theory; he questioned Lizzie about the murders relentlessly. He told newspapers that "recent investigations show that Mrs. Halliday is in all probability connected with the famous Whitechapel murders. It has been proved that she was in Europe at the time. She frequently refers to the subject, both when she is in possession of her mental faculties and when she is raving. Mrs. Halliday is constantly speaking of these murders." Despite Beecher's insistence, there was no proof at all that she had been in Europe in those missing months.

Amidst her talk of the Whitechapel murders, Lizzie allegedly also made reference to the bodies of several other women who had been ripped and disposed of in the Hudson River. Though often her rantings about the murders gave way to an unintelligible ramble, her constant talk about the Ripper crimes on top of the pressing questions of the inquest led those who listened to her to believe that she was in some way related to the case. When Lizzie claimed the Ripper had moved to New York, they were not sure whether she was referring to herself, or just fixated on someone she knew who may have been the killer.

One suspect in the London murders neatly answered Lizzie's ravings. Dr. Francis J. Tumblety—called the "most important suspect to surface" in contemporary debates about the killer—was known in the United States as a "quack doctor and charlatan." His products included the "Tumblety Pimple Destroyer" and "Dr. Morse's Indian Root Pills," and he was often just ahead of the law. Tumblety was even arrested on suspicion of involvement in the Lincoln assassination. His misogyny was extreme; he "savagely denounced all women, especially prostitutes" and often called them "cattle," and he kept "large wardrobe-size cases containing anatomical specimens; over half of them contained uteri from 'every class of woman.'"

He moved to England from New York and was "constantly brought under the notice of police." Arrested and initially suspected of the Whitechapel murders, Scotland Yard had a large dossier on him, but there was not enough evidence to charge him for the crimes. Tumblety then escaped England and, since he had only been charged with misdemeanors, could not be extradited back. This man, who arrived in New York State around the time that Lizzie did, was a more likely suspect for the killings in London.

Despite all theories to the contrary, the murders of Jack the

Ripper bore no resemblance to those of Lizzie Halliday. Her motivation, targets, and methods could hardly have differed more from the Ripper's. She had far more in common with his many victims than with any of those suspected of perpetrating their murders. Lizzie herself put it best when accused of the crime by the sheriff: "What am, I? An elephant? A man did those."

N ellie Bly and the *New York World* wanted an interview. Whether the speculation, however specious, that Lizzie Halliday was Jack the Ripper grabbed the reporter's attention, or simply that her time undercover on Blackwell's Island made "the worst woman in the world" an obvious exclusive, Bly pursued the story. Lizzie Halliday had many visitors during her time in jail and throughout her trial, but none as famous as Nellie Bly.

Photograph of Nellie Bly, 1887.

Since her undercover assignment on Blackwell's, Bly's articles continued to be front-page material, including her recent interview with the anarchist political activist Emma Goldman. She pursued stories and adventures unthinkable for a woman at the time, including reporting from the Eastern Front in WWI and following the fictional journey of Phileas Fogg in Jules Verne's *Around the World in Eighty Days*. Bly did it in seventy-two. A "new journalist," more than eighty years before the exploits of Tom Wolfe or Hunter S. Thompson gave meaning to the phrase, Bly attempted in her reporting "to right wrongs, to explain the unexplored, to satisfy curiosity about the intriguing, to expose unfairness, or to catch a thief." In this story, she wanted to catch a murderer.

Lizzie Halliday was a tough nut to crack, though. Other reporters had tried and failed: "everyone speaks to her: none gets replies." But none of the other reporters had posed as a madwoman on Blackwell's Island. If anyone could get Lizzie to talk, it would be Bly.

When she arrived in October 1893, Bly was struck by the beauty of Monticello, with its "little grassy knoll that faces and forms part" of the town's park, and the contrast between the bucolic picture of the area and the crimes of the woman jailed there. She noted "the wide, unbarred windows and open door of the handsome gray-stone county jail" and the "cheery, little sitting-room."

Sheriff Beecher took the reporter to the prisoner and remained in their company the entirety of that first interview, often interjecting and encouraging Lizzie when Bly asked a challenging question or pushed for an answer. Bly described Lizzie's attitude as "one of rigid expectation and resentment," and Lizzie, at first, refused to acknowledge her presence or respond to her.

Bly took in every detail of the woman and the cell and studied the killer's appearance: "Her hair was very fine and of exquisite red-gold tint . . . almost like a delicate, changeable silk." "Her fat neck was as white as milk" and "her white hands were as spotless as if she had never done any labor." Bly was fascinated by Lizzie's hands, likely considering what they had been used to do, calling them "fat and very thick through." She compared their shape to those of John L. Sullivan, an Irish-American bare-knuckle boxer of the time and remarked on the apparent care and attention that Lizzie gave them.

Oddly, the cell contained an old-fashioned four-poster bed with a "comically fat mattress and bright patchwork quilt." Fore-shadowing Lizzie's attempt only a month later to burn the jail down, Bly also took note of the stove: "as there is no other way of heating, I suppose they must take what little risk there is of a prisoner setting the place on fire, or introducing a keeper into kingdom come with the stove-lid."

Drawing of Lizzie in her jail cell, 1893.

Lizzie had pasted on the walls a "great number of colored

prints from weekly periodicals." Beside the window where she sat was a "full-length picture of a retiring creature in extremely scant garments," who was, according to the caption, "Pauline Bradshaw, of Buffalo, and who left her wealthy husband for the glamour of the stage." Next to it were more pictures of Bradshaw in "remarkable undress . . . diving, perching on rocks and lounging in the sand." Over the windowsill was a copy of the *New York World*, with the headline, "Successful Women Adventuresses." Bly does not editorialize or speculate on the meaning of these pictures, what they meant to Lizzie, or why she would hang them.

When Bly addressed Lizzie, the woman ignored her, staring down at her lap. Sheriff Beecher told his prisoner, "She won't hurt you, Lizzie. Just look up and see how kind she is." Bly narrated the encounter in the article published on October 22, 1893:

> I reached forth my hand and clasped her thick white hand that is said to have sent at least four souls into eternity. Her hand, damp with the claminess produced by a great nervous strain, lay rigidly passive under mine. Still I did not move away, but gently pressed the hand I touched. Then a solitary tear-drop fell on my wrist. Then another. A sudden shower quickly followed the first drops, and Lizzie Halliday, with the back of her hands, hastily and roughly brushed them away.

Bly would not see this vulnerability again throughout the days she spent with her. Lizzie grew suspicious and exhibited both the calculation and strange dissociation that others had experienced.

"How do I know who you are?" Lizzie demanded. "I don't want people coming here telling lies about me. I don't like people comin' here to question me. How do I know who they are or what they want?"

Bly thought that there was nothing insane about her actions, that they were the actions of a "very shrewd person, who was thoroughly conscious of her danger, and was carefully considering all chances before venturing to commit herself in any way."

She was surprised at the sudden turn in Lizzie, as well as her own reaction to it: "what little liking that may have been born by the knowledge of her friendless condition, and, I might as well confess it, the tear that fell upon my hand, vanished abruptly, leaving a decided chill of aversion in its place. No one can look in Lizzie Halliday's face when it wears that expression of cunning speculation and like her."

What Nellie Bly saw was likely what Lizzie's victims saw. "One glance of her countenance can kill every spark of friendliness in the kindest heart that ever throbbed. Robert Louis Stevenson made people experience a thrill of repulsion and fear at the sight of Mr. Hyde's frightful features. How much stranger is it, then, that the sight of this woman's face . . . should freeze the blood of one's veins and banish all feeling of human sympathy."

Pushing hard for a confession, Bly asked her about the murders, about her memory of the time before the murders. Lizzie withheld details and answered vaguely.

"I did not know anything. I wasn't in my right mind."

Bly pushed. "But you can recall what happened before the murder?"

"Everything seems sort of hazy," Lizzie said. "My head hurts me yet. I'm not well."

"She has been out of her mind, you know," the sheriff added, and Bly thought that Lizzie Halliday looked pleased.

Still, she worked hard to get a confession from the woman.

"Did you or did you not kill those people?"

"I have been crazy; I was drugged," Lizzie insisted.

"Tell me," Bly said, "you did it yourself?"

Lizzie turned to the sheriff. "What shall I say, dear?"

"Are you guilty or innocent? Tell me now. I may be able to help you. Anyway I am going away, and you will never see me again."

"Some other time. My head feels bad now. Some other time," said Lizzie.

Within two weeks, however, "Lizzie Halliday sent word through the sheriff that she wanted to see Bly again and tell her everything." When Bly arrived, Lizzie told the reporter that she now remembered everything. Instead of confessing to the crimes, though, Lizzie blamed them on a gang "that make a business of killing and robbing." But mixed in with the tangled tales of the gang were startling details of the murders.

When asked what the gang had done with the bodies of those they had killed, Lizzie responded that "they were put in a barn and burned up. Wood was piled on the embers to burn up every bit of them so there would be nothing left to tell the story." She added that the gang "got insurance on the barn as well as the money they murdered for."

She described how Paul's son had been killed, again attributing it to the gang. "Three fires were built in the house, one in the cellar, one on the first floor, and one on the top floor. The crazy boy was pushed inside, the door was locked and he was burned to death."

Perhaps understanding that Lizzie wanted to talk about the crimes but wasn't going to provide a direct confession, Bly cleverly asked leading questions like "How was the murdering usually done?"

In one account, Lizzie said that the victims "were drugged and shot and their bodies cut up into pieces the largest not being more than a pound." She volunteered that peddlers were often offered drugged whiskey, undressed and shot, and then wrapped completely in cloth and disposed of in the lead mines.

When Bly asked where they were shot, Lizzie put her hand over her heart and answered, "where it would do the most good. . . . They were always shot in the heart, and many times, to make a sure job."

Bly asked Lizzie directly why she had killed the McQuillan women. "I was outside, looking in the window," Lizzie told her. "I had nothing to do with it."

Then Lizzie went on to describe the killing of the women. "They moaned a great deal, so I knew they weren't dead. But enough shots were put in at last to finish them."

Bly continued her indirect approach. "I should have thought that with such wholesale killing the shanty would have been swimming blood."

Lizzie's answers were specific and incriminating. "Sometimes when people are drugged they don't bleed at all. To guard against the blood horse blankets are placed under them, and if there is any blood it soaks into the blankets."

Over the course of the interview, Bly got Lizzie to describe her crimes in detail, from the murders of John and Paul to those of the McQuillan women and the innumerable peddlers that had the misfortune to walk the roads near the Halliday farm. Nonetheless, Lizzie continued to deny committing the crimes herself.

Finally, Bly pressed Lizzie, looking for the clear confession, "You know all these murders so well, but you did not commit them?"

"No; I could not help myself. I watched through the window and saw the gang do it."

This contradictory answer was as close as Bly got to a confession. Still, where no other had succeeded, Bly was able to get Lizzie not only to speak to her but to provide details of her murders and a glimpse into the mind and behavior of a serial killer. But no one, not even Bly, knew that Lizzie Halliday wasn't finished killing.

At the end of the interview, in one last attempt to get a confession from Lizzie Halliday, Bly told her that she would give her $200 for her defense if Lizzie told her the truth.

She grabbed Bly's wrist, with what Bly described as "an eagerness that froze my blood. When I started to go she caught my dress and drew me back."

With the help of the sheriff, Nellie Bly was able to leave Lizzie's cell. When they were outside, the sheriff said, "I never was afraid of her until I saw the gleam that came into her eyes when you showed her that money."

Nellie Bly would never visit again, having gotten as close to the truth as she could from Lizzie's ramblings and stories. Her coverage of the murderer continued her streak of front-page stories, each stretching across several columns on the front of the Sunday edition of the *New York World*. Only a few weeks after Bly's last visit, Lizzie would begin her own streak of jailhouse violence, starting with the attempt to strangle the sheriff's wife.

She would have to wait until the following summer for her day in court. On June 9, 1894, in Monticello, the entire courthouse in the usually peaceful seat of Sullivan County buzzed with the chatter of people fascinated by the case about to be tried there. Locals and travelers from surrounding areas alike, demanding access to a seat at the hottest show in town, swanned about the courthouse, dressed in their finery. They were not shy to socialize, even at such a solemn occasion. The entire scene may have looked more like a county fair than a murder trial.

People brought their children to witness Lizzie Halliday with hopes of seeing the crazy behavior they'd read about. For many the horrors about to be recounted were all too real—for some, the man and the women murdered were friends, family, neighbors. Reporters flocked in from as far away as Los Angeles, looking for sensational revelations and episodes to thrill millions of readers throughout the United States. Dispatches from the trial of Lizzie

Halliday would reach as far as England and Kingston, Jamaica. This was international news.

The courthouse in Monticello, NY.

Lizzie Halliday stood in a courtroom for the third time since she had met Paul Halliday; the charges she faced more serious than they had ever been. Instead of stealing horses or arson, she was accused of murdering three people, and there was solid evidence to convict her.

In her lawyer, Lizzie was fortunate. George Carpenter was "not a rural pettifogger, but a lawyer of more than ordinary talent, and has frequently been identified with intricate criminal litigation." There was very little question, especially given Lizzie's former incarceration in the Matteawan Hospital for the Criminally Insane, that she would be pleading not guilty by reason of insanity to all three murders. Observers in court, as most who came into contact with Lizzie Halliday did, questioned whether she was actually insane. Her behavior was inconsistent. At times she would seem perfectly lucid, only to strike out in a sudden violent rage, or to begin babbling incoherently. The answer to this question would determine her fate.

The question of her motivation—especially in the death of the McQuillans—also aroused debate. District Attorney Hill would work to prove a connection between Lizzie Halliday and the two women she murdered: Margaret McQuillan and her daughter, Sarah. Through even rudimentary forensic knowledge, it was easy enough for the prosecution to prove that Paul Halliday had died a significant length of time before the McQuillans, so he could not have been the killer. What motivated a wife to kill her husband might not have seemed especially mysterious, particularly after details of their tumultuous marriage and her prior behavior came out. Understanding what caused her to target two women from a town miles away was a different matter. How did she convince them to come to the farm? Why did she kill them?

Two officers led Lizzie into the courtroom. Wearing a "plain brown dress," she stared at the floor, avoiding the eyes of the crowd. She was pale and, over the course of the two-day trial, the strain on her was evident. At one point, her "head fell upon her breast and she shivered." One reporter wrote that it would "be a miracle if she does not break down." Her behavior would be strange throughout the trial.

Out of the fifty-three jurors interviewed, three were chosen. Two farmers and a carpenter would decide Lizzie's fate. Three principal questions were posed to the jurors: "Have you any prejudice against circumstantial evidence?"; "Have you any prejudice against capital punishment?"; Have you any prejudices or objection against the defense of insanity?"

Her lawyer immediately moved to rest the case on a plea of insanity, but District Attorney Hill maintained that he could prove both intent and sanity. In an opening address that lasted less than thirty minutes, the prosecutor argued the weight of the circumstantial evidence. There were no eyewitnesses to the crimes, so Hill called a series of witnesses to build the story of what happened over the course of those weeks in which Paul Halliday and Margaret and Sarah McQuillan died.

Hill's first witness placed Lizzie in Newburgh "looking for domestic help" and saw Margaret McQuillan leave town with her. Within the week, Lizzie returned and convinced Sarah to leave with her, telling the woman that her mother had "fallen from a stepladder and hurt herself." Others testified to seeing Lizzie with the McQuillans, strengthening the chain. Hill would call twenty-five witnesses.

Then Thomas McQuillan, husband to Margaret and father to Sarah, was called. The courtroom was silent as he took the stand. Lizzie had come to the house and offered Margaret two dollars a day for a month's work. Then she returned for his daughter, telling them that Margaret had broken her leg and wanted Sarah to "come and care for her." He sent his daughter off with Lizzie and never saw her again. Thomas McQuillan broke down in tears. The defense declined to cross-examine.

Through the testimonies of other witnesses, the women's clothing and jewelry were identified, and the results of the searches were introduced. The prosecution produced the murder weapon and, in a dangerously comic moment, the judge learned five of the chambers were loaded. He ordered it unloaded "before further damage was done."

Then one of Paul's sons took the stand as likely the last person besides Lizzie to see Paul Halliday alive. He told the court of the events of that week, the path to the search warrant, and of Lizzie's threat to the constable to "cut his heart's blood out" the day of the search. The details of the murders began to fall into place.

Using the gun Paul had borrowed to protect himself from her, Lizzie shot him in the chest three times, beat his face in with a club, and then buried him under the floorboards of the house. Why she did it, what spurred her at that particular time to kill Paul, was and is a mystery. Was the mere presence of a gun in the house enough of an inducement or a temptation to murder him?

Days after his death, she went to Newburgh looking for housekeeping help, possibly to clean up the murder scene. If the details of Bly's interview with Lizzie can be trusted, Margaret said, "My God! Did you bring me here to murder me?" After shooting the woman, Lizzie went for her daughter. She may have drugged the McQuillans before killing them, a seemingly out of character act of mercy.

Lizzie's lawyer did not put her on the stand and "made no effort to combat the circumstantial evidence," relying instead on the plea of insanity. He called only six witnesses. With eyes "half closed," Lizzie picked constantly at her handkerchief and the sleeves of her dress. When George Carpenter called the deputy sheriff who arrested her for stealing the wagon and horses, the man told the court that "she was as wild as a hawk" and, in his opinion, "she was insane then." Sheriff Beecher echoed that opinion when he took the stand. "When she came to me," he said, "she was without any intelligence, filthy in her habits and talked to imaginary people."

Carpenter called three doctors for the defense, one of them the superintendent of the Matteawan Hospital for the Criminally Insane and another her attending physician when she was institutionalized in Middletown State Hospital. They all told the jury that Lizzie was "hopelessly insane."

The next morning, the prosecution's doctors performed an examination on Lizzie Halliday in her cell. She was "gently forced down" into a chair, but leaped at one of the physicians, kicking him in the lower abdomen. The district attorney caught her by the throat. She tried to bite him. Once restrained, another physician checked her "pulse, hair, flesh, and eyes." Screaming, she butted the district attorney with her head and escaped to the floor, "kicking, yelling, biting and hurling epithets at her captors."

Less than an hour later, Lizzie was taken back into the courtroom while a crowd picnicked under the trees outside in the fair June weather. On the stand, the doctors declared that she was not insane. One said, "she is shamming, and is overdoing the part." During the five-minute examination, "she told him that her age was 'nineteen skunks,' her residence was 'I washed your shirt,' and her father's name was 'you took my property.'" Under Carpenter's cross examination, the doctor said that one way he knew Lizzie was faking was that "she had no horizontal wrinkles on her forehead." Another doctor testified that he "had found her hair soft, oily and natural, and that she perspired naturally and that these facts indicated sanity."

With the opinions of the doctors fresh in the jury's ears, the trial moved to closing statements. The jury quickly returned a guilty verdict, but her sentence—life or death—would still hang on the question of Lizzie Halliday's sanity.

On the morning of her sentencing, Lizzie ate beefsteak and onions, drank a cup of tea, and nibbled at a piece of cake. In no mood to talk, she refused to answer when asked how she was feeling. When she was taken into the courtroom, "the usual questions were put to her, but she answered none" and "her body swayed in the grasp of the officers." The jury declared Lizzie sane.

George Carpenter watched his client with "sincere pity showing in his face." When the judge condemned Lizzie to death in the electric chair, "tears streamed down his face." Lizzie "rubbed her nose and stroked her chin," and there was some doubt as to whether she was fully aware of what was happening. She was led out "without a sign of recognition of the terrible sentence."

But when she reached her cell, she refused to go in and had to be "forced along by the sheriff." In the following days, she was "very belligerent" and "tried to fight those who approached her." She worked to break her leg chain.

Despite her previous fondness for him, she even bit the hand of the sheriff, Harrison Beecher, as hard as she could. The sheriff, anticipating such a violent attack from Lizzie, was prepared with gloved hands to fend off whatever she threw at him, but her bite was so gleefully hard that her teeth broke through the heavy material of his glove and badly wounded his hand. Later, the wound infected his hand, which swelled so badly that doctors feared he might have to lose his whole arm. Lizzie registered her reaction to her sentence of death by electrocution in her usual language of violence.

The electric chair was still new. It had been used for the first time in 1890, only four years earlier—and never to execute a woman. "Electrocide" was conceived of by a commission formed by the New York governor David B. Hill in 1885 as a humane alternative to hanging. The members of the commission were a lawyer, a "law expert," and a dentist. The wonder over the new method and the promise of a "certain, swift, and painless" death prompted novelist William Dean Howells to say sarcastically that this "killing by electricity was almost the same as not killing at all." The reality of an execution by electricity was far different.

The chair's first occupant, William Kemmler, repeatedly told the warden to "take your time. Don't be in a hurry." The warden reassured him that it wouldn't hurt. The electrodes were wetted, one placed on the condemned man's head and the other at the base of his spine. After final checks of the chair, the electric current was switched on. Kemmler's body spasmed and "remained rigid for seventeen seconds." Believing the man was dead, the electricity was turned off. His finger contracted and, realizing Kemmler was still alive, a doctor called for the current to be turned back on. But the voltmeter "registered an almost imperceptible current." They worked to regain the electricity while the man suffered for over a minute. When the current returned, they kept it going for over four minutes at two thousand volts. A white vapor rose from the body, "bearing with it the pungent and sickening odor of a body burning." The men rushed to shut off the electricity. This was not the quick or cruelty-free execution that the new technology promised.

That first electric chair was partially bankrolled by Thomas Edison in an attempt to prove how dangerous Nikola Tesla and George Westinghouse's alternating current (AC) was, compared with his preferred direct current (DC). He would go so far as to electrocute a circus elephant in Coney Island to make his point.

Many believed that Lizzie should be spared from this new tool of state-sanctioned execution. Her defense filed an application almost immediately after her sentencing to reevaluate her sanity. Swayed by public opinion, the governor of New York, Roswell P. Flower, opened an inquest into the prisoner's mental state. If she was, in fact, insane, a civil society could not hold her accountable for her actions, rampantly bloody as they were. Meanwhile, she was sent to Dannemora state prison to await execution.

By mid-July, the commission was finished. Their opinion was equivocal and part of the memorandum read:

> The defense was insanity, and the evidence to establish it was very strong. Dr. Selden H. Talcott, Medical Supervisor of the Middletown State Hospital, and Dr. Henry E. Allison, Medical Superintendent of the Matteawan State Hospital, both of them men of great experience, testified that she had at different times, some years before the homicide, been under their charge as an insane patient, at which times she was unquestionably insane, and that they had no doubt she was insane at the time of the homicide.

The commission contended that there was "little question that she is really insane, but that the local feeling was very bitter against her, and the jury was no doubt influenced by this." As they determined she was "not a fit subject for the death penalty," they recommended commutation of the sentence to life imprisonment.

Lizzie's life was spared. She would not follow William Kemmler into death via the electric chair. The first woman to die in the electric chair would actually be the third woman sentenced to it. The second, Maria Barbella, had been convicted of murdering her lover who had drugged and raped her. She was pardoned. Martha Place, a tiny woman, who had murdered her seventeen-year-old stepdaughter Ida by throwing a vat of acid in her eyes and smothering her with a pillow, then attacked her husband with an ax when he returned home, was the first woman to die by the new scientific method. She did not make a sound in the electric chair and in two quick shocks, her life was over. This was the fate that Lizzie Halliday narrowly avoided when her plea of insanity, the same plea that spared Maria Barbella and was not enough to save Martha Place, was accepted.

Lizzie was, instead, sent back to the Matteawan Hospital for the Criminally Insane. But the next few years would not be quiet ones. Lizzie's formidable and unregulated spirit would not be subdued within its walls.

P eople in the Catskills region of New York State will recognize the Matteawan Hospital for the Criminally Insane as the Fishkill Correctional Facility. It's no longer a mental institution and hasn't been since the mid-seventies. In addition to Lizzie Halliday, notable inmates included George Metesky, New York City's "Mad Bomber"; Valerie Solanas, the woman who attempted to murder Andy Warhol; Harry Thaw who succeeded in murdering Stanford White; and Izola Ware Curry, the African American woman who attempted to assassinate Martin Luther King, Jr.

Matteawan Hospital for the Criminally Insane.

New York opened its first state institution for the insane in 1843. The Utica Lunatic Asylum housed both patients from the community, many of whom had entered voluntarily, and violent and escape-prone prisoners from jails and prisons. The challenge of housing both and the danger posed to "civil patients" led to the opening in 1859 of the State Lunatic Asylum for Insane Convicts for convicted prisoners who exhibited signs of mental illness. But the Utica Lunatic Asylum was still responsible for "those too insane to stand trial and those acquitted by reason of insanity." The second facility did not solve the original problem of housing the nonviolent and violent together.

The other challenge was that there were few ways to reduce the population. Before the State Care Act of 1890, people whose sentences had expired, but who were still considered insane, were often discharged into the custody of county poorhouses or "almshouses." But after 1890, overcrowding became severe.

The building of the Matteawan Hospital for the Criminally Insane was one solution. The state purchased 246 acres of farmland in the village of Matteawan for $25,000, and Isaac Perry, the architect for the New York State Capitol, drew up plans for buildings with "an abundance of light and ventilation." In April 1892, the new facility opened with room for 550 patients. Only seven years later, another prison mental hospital would open because these additional 550 beds were not nearly enough.

Matteawan was at the time headed by Harry E. Allison, the medical doctor who had overseen Lizzy's previous stay at Matteawan and was able to vouch for her insanity at the time of her crimes. Whereas Blackwell's Island was known for its inhumane conditions, particularly after Nellie Bly's scathing exposé, the facility in the Hudson Valley purported to offer "kind and gentle treatment in a stress-free, highly routine environment," with "occupational therapy": "cooking, maintenance, farming and making baskets, rugs, clothing and bedsheets." In reality, though not on the inhumane scale of Blackwell's Island, the facility was understaffed and overcrowded.

Lizzie Halliday's first attempt at serious violence after her incarceration came a couple of years after she entered Matteawan. Outraged by how the staff on the ward treated her, she repeatedly requested to be transferred to another prison. Lizzie's demands went unheard. So, she gained attention the only way that had worked for her before: attempted murder.

She and another inmate conspired to strangle a nurse named Catherine Ward. Following her into the bathroom, they jumped on her and crammed a towel in her mouth. Lizzie tore at her hair and scratched her face, then they choked her. By the time they were stopped, Ward was unconscious and feared dead. Catherine Ward survived, but a week later, still showed the marks of Lizzie Halliday's fingers on her throat. The medical head of the hospital dismissed this attack as a hazard of working at the hospital that could have come from any one of the 750 inmates at the time. He said that all of the staff was trained to expect violence like this, and they knew how to react against it in a way that was safe both for them and for the residents of the hospital.

Lizzie attempted escape at least once, according to the account of a young German woman named Ottila Schneider, who became the first woman to successfully escape Matteawan, upon which she fled back to Germany. Lizzie found her own street clothes and, dressed in them, joined a group of visitors to the asylum. She made it to every door but the last, when she was caught by a guard and returned to the ward.

Lizzie didn't confine her wiles to escape or violence either. Ever vigilant for financial gain, she attempted to exploit a loophole in pension laws by applying for Paul Halliday's soldier's pension as his widow. In May 1901, she filed a claim "notwithstanding the fact that she became a widow by murdering her husband." A local pension attorney, Col. W. L. Delacy, confirmed that, under the 1890 law, she was entitled to Halliday's pension, as it "excluded only the widows of those who commit suicide."

Lizzie Halliday died of natural causes at the age of fifty-four on June 18, 1918, and was buried in an unmarked grave on the grounds of the Matteawan hospital. But not before she killed one last time.

11

Twenty-one-year-old nursing attendant Nellie Wickes entered the Matteawan Hospital for the Criminally Insane for her last day of work on September 27, 1906. She'd moved to the institution from her family home in Bay Shore to begin her nursing career. Technically, as Matteawan housed the criminally insane, she wasn't just a nursing attendant, but a corrections officer, as well. She had worked there for a year, but it was time to move on. The world was changing; doors were opening for women. She was going to pursue a degree in nursing.

Beloved by both the staff and the patients, Wickes had been appointed head attendant of her ward the past January. One of the patients, Lizzie Halliday, was particularly upset that Nurse Nellie would be leaving. A week prior, Wickes had given the forty-two-year-old Irish woman the news. "If you try to leave me," Lizzie said, "I will kill you."

In the moment, Wickes laughed. "Oh, I guess not," she said. "You wouldn't harm me." But she must have known of Lizzie Halliday's attempt years earlier to strangle a nurse on the ward.

On that last day of work at Matteawan, Wickes said goodbye to Lizzie. "Try not to make any trouble," she told her patient.

Halliday said, "You'd better not try it!"

That morning, Wickes took a short break from her rounds and detoured toward the bathroom. She walked quickly, careful not to be gone too long. The other staff reported to her that whenever she left the room, Lizzie would tap her foot impatiently, growing more and more visibly agitated until her favorite nurse returned. Wickes was aware of Lizzie's long history of self-harm and violent mania that could be triggered by such an intense change.

She walked as quickly as she could down the hallway toward the bathroom and did not, at first, realize that she was being followed. When she heard footsteps moving more quickly than her own right behind her, though, Wickes paused with her hand on the door to the bathroom and turned. There was Lizzie Halliday, not five paces away from her. Within seconds, Lizzie was upon her, snarling and spitting as she opened the door to the bathroom and shoved the nurse inside.

OCTOBER 17, 1906.

MURDER BY A MANIAC

Lizzie Halliday, Ex-Gypsy, Adds a Seventh Victim to Her List.

STABS NURSE WITH SHEARS

Horrible Crime of Crazy Woman in Hospital For Insane Criminals at Matteawan, N. Y.

SHE BEGAN STABBING HER VICTIM.

Newspaper illustration of the murder of Nellie Wickes, 1906.

Wickes fought as hard as she could to release the death grip that Lizzie Halliday had on her throat, but in the end, she was no match for her patient. Lizzie threw her onto the floor, fumbling for the keys strapped to Wickes' nursing belt. She locked the door from the inside so that the attendants outside could not stop her. Then, with the shears she pulled from the nurse's belt, Lizzie began to stab the woman in her face, neck, chest, and breasts.

The attack lasted only a few minutes before the attendants were able to produce a duplicate key, unlock the door, and pull the violent woman off the nurse. But in those moments, Wickes had been stabbed over two hundred times. Blood soaked the bathroom floor. Her face was nearly unrecognizable. Despite the best efforts of a hospital full of doctors, her shallow breathing lasted only two more hours before Nellie Wickes died.

Epilogue

Blackwell's Island, Middletown, Matteawan. The fin-de-siècle insane asylum was a link in the chain connecting the murderer Lizzie Halliday, the investigative reporter Nellie Bly and the unfortunate Nellie Wickes, the nurse-jailer who Lizzie stabbed to death in a bathroom. The women are like facets of a prism: look to any one of them and get a different angle on madness, and society's answer to it.

Women, in particular, were routinely incarcerated in insane asylums for the crimes of being independent-minded, or poor, or simply in the way. Some of Nellie Bly's companions on the boat trip to Blackwell's may not have been insane at all.

Defining insanity, especially in the context of the criminal justice system, has always been rife with problems. The definition is continually evolving, and diagnosis has been radically inconsistent. The legal question is whether the defendant is responsible for her actions, or at the mercy of episodic or persistent mental illness. Was Lizzie Halliday feigning madness to avoid prison? Is there a difference between an irrational, erratic killer and a rational, calculating one? Are both insane? In her particular brand of madness, Lizzie nonetheless demonstrated a will to self-determination that she shared with the two Nellies.

Nellie Bly was remarkable not just for her drive for independence, which many women possessed, but also for her ability to actualize it. Whatever Nellie Bly wanted to do, it seemed, Nellie Bly did.

Nellie Wickes represented just the kind of independence Nellie Bly had trailblazed and a new generation of women was chasing. Having taken one step toward self-determination by working at Matteawan, Nellie Wickes was poised to take another when Lizzie's will to keep her near ended her life. That improvements in asylum conditions spurred by Nellie Bly's articles may have paved Lizzie's murderous way is a terrible irony. Wickes was the first female officer in the United States killed in the line of duty, a distinction nobody would ever have chosen.

The tragedy of Lizzie Halliday lay in her twisted, psychopathic version of such self-determination. Lizzie, too, acted upon her desires, not by traveling around the world, or getting a front-page byline (though she got her fair share of front-page coverage), or even by becoming a nurse, but by marrying where she could and murdering at every turn. The innumerable bodies of her victims seeded the Catskill Mountains. When society attempted to contain her in a cell or a ward, Lizzie responded in the only way she knew, with violence and more murder. Whether from madness or malevolence or a combination of both, she exerted her indomitable will, leaving a catalog of grisly deaths and an ignoble legacy behind.

A Word From C.J. March

Thank you for reading *Murderer's Gulch*. If you have thoughts on this book or suggestions for other true crime accounts, please let us know at cjmarch@deadtruecrime.com. We love hearing from readers. You're why we write.

Sign up for our mailing list to learn about new Dead True Crime books and to read and listen to a free, exclusive story: www. deadtruecrime.com/ebook.

If you're interested in reading more about Lizzie Halliday, check out the bibliography at the end of the book.

Other Dead True Crime Books

Sacrificial Axe
Voodoo Cult Slayings in the Deep South

The "Axe-man" came in the night. No one heard him come. No locks could keep him out. In the morning, whole families lay slaughtered in their beds, a riot of blood corrupting the room. Town by town, terror gripped the black communities of Louisiana and East Texas, as men, women, and children fell to the killer's ax. The police were powerless to stop it. Was it simply a homicidal maniac on the loose, or was a deeper evil afoot? Could one person perpetrate over forty atrocities? Was the serial killer even a man? People whispered voodoo, and white newspapers in the Jim Crow era South fanned the hysteria. As the police slowly unraveled the mystery, they were stunned by the bizarre truth of the "Axe-man."

Get Sacrificial Axe

Ghoul of Grays Harbor: Murder and Mayhem in the Pacific Northwest

Sailors trusted him with their money and their lives. That was a mistake. The lucky ones woke up with headaches in the holds of ships headed to China. The others never took another breath.

Billy Gohl robbed, 'shanghaied,' and killed sailors across the Pacific Northwest. Grays Harbor in Aberdeen, Washington was so full of bodies that newspapers dubbed it a 'floaters fleet.' His trapdoor of death was famous. In his time, Gohl murdered over 100 people, making him one of the most prolific serial killers in American history.

Get Ghoul of Grays Harbor

Poison Widow

Arsenic Murders in the Jazz Age

First, she predicts your death. Then, you die. Usually, writhing in pain. Is she a fortune teller, or something much, much darker? Nobody tells the police, not for a long time, because, well, nobody in Chicago's Little Warsaw wants to cross Tillie Klimek. The body count racks up as Jazz Age Chicago's most notorious female poisoner takes down husband after husband, and some other relatives while she's at it. Few, it seems, can resist Tillie's cooking. But is this Mrs. Bluebeard working alone? Or is she part of a bigger, more diabolical "poison trust"? And can Chicago's Finest get to her before her latest husband, already mortally ill, dies? *Poison Widow* is a true-crime aficionado's feast, arsenic-laced and stuffed with tasty noir morsels.

Get Poison Widow

Killer Genius

The Bizarre Case of the Homicidal Scholar

He's a doctor whose patients have a way of dying; a lawyer, who uses his skills to squirm out of criminal convictions. He's a scholar, but other scholars have no idea what he's talking about. He's a family man, but one day, his wife and baby disappear forever. Only two things are clear: Edward Rulloff is a mystery, and everywhere he goes, death and destruction follow. While the criminal justice system has its hands full trying to keep and convict Edward Rulloff, the world will argue whether he's a genius, a scam artist or a madman. Even Mark Twain has an opinion.

Get Killer Genius

Coming Soon

Exit Row
Mass Murder in the Canadian Sky

A clear day. An experienced pilot. A routine flight. An obsessive love-triangle. What could go wrong? When a mysterious package follows J. Albert Guay's wife on board Flight 108, calamity is just a few ticks of the clock away. How far will a man go for his adulterous passion?

Cannibal Cowboy
Murder and Man-Eating on the American Frontier

Gold Rush and gunfights, scalping and saloons, the Old West had a reputation to uphold. But even the rough and tumble frontier wasn't ready for the likes of the Kentucky Cannibal. Mountain man and gunfighter Boone Helm would do anything to survive, right down to eating his enemies. Or his friends.

Blood Trade
Slaughter on the Underground Railroad

Nothing could be worse than slavery. Unless it was Patty Cannon hunting you down. A gang of thugs at her command, the woman infamous for her blood-thirst and brutality murdered free blacks and fugitive slaves alike for decades. Working her illegal slave trade in what became known as the Reverse Underground Railroad, Cannon's grisly tactics still have the power to chill centuries later.

About the Author

C.J. March is the alter ego of three true crime enthusiasts who wanted to write the kind of juicy noir histories they like to read. Between them they have: 2 MFAs, 3 arrests, 4 folk albums, 73 years of therapy, 1 stint working for "the artist formerly known as" which ended in a shoving match, 40 years of writing, 30 years of design, 3 dogs, and 1 overnight in a cell with a murderer.

A Note On Names

Over the course of her life, Lizzie Halliday was known by the last name of her father and by the last names of several husbands. For the sake of clarity, Lizzie Halliday is frequently referred to as "Lizzie" in the book, instead of by a last name.

Bibliography

"Another Account: Details of the Execution." *Los Angeles Times*, August 7, 1890.

Armitage, David, Alison Bashford, and Sujit Sivasundaram, eds. *Oceanic Histories*. Cambridge: Cambridge University Press, 2018.

Bly, Nellie. *Ten Days in a Mad-House*. New York: Ian L. Munro, 1887.

"The Burlingham Murders." *New York Times*, September 6, 1893.

"Commutation of Mrs. Halliday's Sentence." *Boston Medical and Surgical Journal* 131, no. 4 (July 26, 1894): 94.

"Coney Elephant Killed." *New York Times*, January 5, 1903.

Conway, John. *Remembering the Sullivan County Catskills*. Stroud, UK: The History Press, 2008.

"The Crime of a Decade: Story of the Horrible Murders Perpetrated by Mrs. Lizzie Halliday." *Minneapolis Tribune*, September 15, 1893.

"Cuts Her Throat with Broken Glass." *Chicago Daily Tribune,* December 12, 1893.

"Defense Begins." *Buffalo Evening News*, June 21, 1894.

"Deep Mrs. Halliday." *On the St. Lawrence and Clayton Independent*, October 27, 1893.

"Distrusted Mrs. Halliday." *New York Times*, September 12, 1893.

"Eliza Halliday - Monster." *New York World,* September 19, 1893

Frommer, Myrna, and Harvey Frommer. *It Happened in the Catskills*. Albany, New York: State University of New York Press, 2009.

Gribben, Arthur. ed. *The Great Famine and the Irish Diaspora in America*. Amherst, Massachusetts: University of Massachusetts Press, 1999.

"Guilty of Murder: A Jack the Ripper in Female Shape to be Electrocuted." *Marion Daily Star*, September 14, 1893.

"The Halliday Murder Case." *New York Times*, September 7, 1893.

"Halliday Murder Trial." *Port Jervis Union*, June 18, 1894.

"Halliday Trial." *Buffalo Evening News*, June 19, 1894.

"Her's a Mania for Murder." *Port Jervis Union*, September 11, 1893.

"Insane Woman Gets Out of Matteawan." *New York Times,* November 22, 1911.

"Is Mrs. Halliday Crazy?" *Port Jervis Union*, October 18, 1893.

"Is Mrs. Halliday Insane" *The Argus*, July 9, 1894.

King, Gilbert. "Edison vs. Westinghouse: A Shocking Rivalry." *Smithsonian*, October 11, 2011. https://www.smithsonianmag.com/history/edison-vs-westinghouse-a-shocking-rivalry-102146036

Kroeger, Brooke. *Nellie Bly: Daredevil. Reporter. Feminist.* New York: Three Rivers Press, 2013.

LaRocca, Charles J. *The 124th New York State Volunteers in the Civil War: A History and Roster*. Jefferson, NC: McFarland & Company, Inc., 2012.

"Lizzie Halliday - Governor Flowers Thinks She is Too Crazy to Be Electrocuted." *Los Angeles Herald*, June 25, 1894.

"Lizzie Halliday Kills Her Nurse." *Kingston Daily Freeman*, September 28, 1906.

"Lizzie Halliday Sent to Dannemora." *Buffalo Evening News*, June 24, 1894.

"Lizzie Halliday Soon to Be Tried." *New York Times*, June 10, 1894.

"Lizzie Halliday, the Murderess, Has Finally Quieted Down." *Chicago Daily Tribune*, September 4, 1895.

"Lizzie Halliday's Bad Temper." *New York Times*, September 2, 1895.

"Mania Like Jack the Ripper." *Roanoke Times*, September 13, 1893.

"Maria Barberi in Role of Heroine." *New York Journal*, December 31, 1896.

"Martha Place Dies in Electric Chair." *San Francisco Call*, March 21, 1899.

Martschukat, Jürgen. "The Art of Killing by Electricity." *Journal of American History* 89, no. 3 (December 2002).

"More About Mrs. Halliday." *Middletown Daily Times*, December 4, 1893.

"Mrs. Halliday in Jail." *New York Times*, September 9, 1893.

"Mrs. Halliday is in Monticello Jail." *Chicago Daily Tribune*, September 9, 1893.

"Mrs. Halliday Seemed Sane." *New York Times*, June 20, 1894.

"Mrs. Halliday Tries to Burn Jail." *New York Times*, November 24, 1893.

"Mrs. Halliday, Insane, Stabs Nurse 200 Times." *New York Times,* September 28, 1906.

"Mrs. Halliday's Case." *Watertown Herald*, October 7, 1893.

"Mrs. Halliday's Case Called." *New York Times*, June 19, 1894.

"Mrs. Halliday's Murders." *The Illustrated American*, October 7, 1893.

"Mrs. Halliday's Trial Begun." *Washington Post*, June 18, 1894.

"Mrs. Halliday's Trial Near at Hand." *New York Times*, June 5, 1894.

"Multimurderess Dies in Asylum." *Washington Post,* June 30, 1918.

"Murdered in Insane Asylum." *Alexandria Gazette*, September 28, 1906.

"A Murderous Maniac: The Many Crimes Charged Against Lizzie Halliday." *Frederick News*, September 11, 1893.

"Nellie Bly Visits Mrs. Halliday." *New York World*, October 22, 1893.

"Paul Halliday's Body Found." *New York Times*, September 8, 1893.

"Pension for Murderess." *Los Angeles Times*, May 8, 1901.

"Poisoned by Mrs. Halliday's Bite. The Sheriff County in Danger of Losing His Arm." *New-York Tribune*, August 25, 1894.

"Refuses to Take Food." *Niagara Falls Gazette*, December 2, 1893.

Rumbelow, Donald. *The Complete Jack the Ripper*. London: Random House, 2013.

"A Second Inquest Held." *New York Times*, September 12, 1893.

"Three Murders Charged Against Mrs. Halliday." *Westfield Republican*, September 13, 1893.

"To Death!" *Buffalo Commercial*, June 22, 1894.

"Treacherous Lizzie Halliday." *Westfield Republican*, November 15, 1893.

"Two Murderous Lunatics." *Washington Post*, September 2, 1895.

"Was Like A Tigress." *New York World*, June 21, 1894.

"The Ways of the Gipsy." *New-York Tribune*, June 10, 1906.

"Weird Life of Crime - Mrs. Halliday's Many Marriages and Murders." *Morning Star*, June 19, 1894.

"A Weird Murderess." *New York World*, June 20, 1894.

Wescott, Tom. *The Bank Holiday Murders: The True Story of the First Whitechapel Murders*. Oklahoma: Crime Confidential Press, 2013.

Wilson, A.J. *Revival: The Business of Insurance*. London: Taylor & Francis, 1904.

"A Woman without a Heart." *New York World*, November 5, 1893.

Image Credits

CHAPTER 1

Hand drawn map of the area surrounding the Halliday farm. Courtesy *New York World*, November 5, 1893.

Newspaper artist drawing of Lizzie Halliday. Courtesy *Huntington Weekly Herald*, December 29, 1893.

CHAPTER 3

Photographs of the barn where McQuillan women were buried. Courtesy *The Illustrated American*, October 7, 1893.

CHAPTER 5

Newspaper engraving of Halliday. Courtesy *The National Police Gazette*, September 13, 1893.

CHAPTER 7

Photograph of Nellie Bly. Courtesy Loc.Gov, Library of Congress.

Drawing of Lizzie in her jail cell. Courtesy *New York World*, October 22, 1893.

CHAPTER 8

The courthouse in Monticello. Courtesy NYCourts.Gov, New York State Unified Court System.

CHAPTER 10

Matteawan Hospital for the Criminally Insane. Courtesy Loc.Gov, Library of Congress.

CHAPTER 11

Slingshot Books
Minneapolis

SLINGSHOT
BOOKS

www.slingshotbooks.com

38146854R00050

Made in the USA
Lexington, KY
04 May 2019